No 2

Then & Now

The Sheffield Blitz

By Alistair Lofthouse

Alistair Lofthouse
DESIGN &
PRINT

© Alistair Lofthouse 2001

Printed and published by:
ALD Design & Print
279 Sharrow Vale Road
Sheffield S11 8ZF

Telephone 0114 267 9402
E:mail a.lofthouse@btinternet.com

ISBN 1-901587-09-6

First published 2001, reprinted 2002, 2003(with updates), 2007 (with updates)

Other titles in the series

Mi-Amigo - The Story of Sheffield's Flying Fortress - David Harvey	ISBN 1-901587-00-2
Tales From a Peak District Bookshop - Mike Smith	ISBN 1-901587-01-0
Tha' Don't look Proper - Anne Hunt	ISBN 1-901587-02-9
Shiny Sheff - The Story of Sheffield's Fighting Ships - Alistair Lofthouse	ISBN 1-901587-03-7
Doug's War - An Erksome Business - Doug Sanderson	ISBN 1-901587-04-5
The Dramatic Story of The Sheffield Flood - Peter Machan	ISBN 1-901584-05-3
Carl Wark - Peak District Fortress or Folly? - Mick Savage	ISBN 1-901587-06-1
Then & Now - Sheffield - Alistair Lofthouse	ISBN 1-901587-07-X
Charlie Peace, The Banner Cross Murderer - Peter Machan	ISBN 1-901587-08-8
They Lived in Sharrow and Nether Edge - Nether Edge Neighbourhood Group	ISBN 1-901587-10-X
Discovering Derbyshire's White Peak - Tom Bates	ISBN 1-901587-11-8
Lost Sheffield - Portrait of a Victorian City - Peter Machan	ISBN 1-901587-12-6
The Sheffield Flood (Large format for schools) - Peter Machan	ISBN 1-901587-13-4
The Sheffield Outrages, The Trade Union Scandals - Peter Machan	ISBN 1-901587-14-2
A Layman's Look at the History, Industry, People and Places of Oughtibridge, Worrall and Wharncliffe Side - Doug Sanderson	ISBN 1-901587-15-0
Derbyshire in Old Photographs - Elizabeth Mottram & Alistair Lofthouse	ISBN 1-901587-16-9
Weerz me dad? 40s & 50s Childhood Stories - Fred Pass-	ISBN 1-901587-17-7
'Orreight mi Ol?' - Don Alexander	ISBN 1-901587-18-5
Sheffield Woodland Detectives (Large Format for Schools) - Joan & Mel Jones	ISBN 1-901587-19-3
The Story of Nether Edge Hospital - Joan Flett	ISBN 1-901587-20-7
More By Luck Than Judgement - Prof. Roy Newton	ISBN 1-901587-21-5
Memories of the Workhouse & Hospital at Fir Vale - Lyn Howsam	ISBN 1-901587-22-3
All Mine - memories of a Bomb & Mine Disposal Officer - Noel Cashford MBE	ISBN 1-901587-23-1
Hanged in Sheffield - David Bentley	ISBN 1-901587-24-X
Club 60 & The Esquire 1960-67 - Sounds of the 60s - Don Hale/Terry Thornton	ISBN 1-901587-26-6
The Story of Sheffield's High Street - Pat Dallman	ISBN 1-902587-27-4

Contents

Dedication

This book is dedicated to
the many people who died during the night of
Thursday 12th December 1940
in the Sheffield Blitz

Foreword

The year 2000 marked the 60th anniversary of the Sheffield Blitz. Today it seems strange to me to see pictures of our own city in ruins. It was for this reason that I decided to take photographs of present scenes for direct comparison with those of the devastation after the Sheffield Blitz.

Sheffield had previously suffered disasters. The Sheffield Blitz was the third major disaster to befall Sheffield. The Sheffield Flood of 1864 killed 250 people when the new Dale Dyke dam burst, flooding much of Victorian Sheffield. The cholera epidemic of 1832 killed around 400 people. More recently we have the Hillsborough disaster in 1989 that accounted for 96 deaths. The night of December 12th 1940, however, was one whose tragic consequences would go down in history.

I have also gathered together the thoughts and memories of some of those who were in Sheffield during the Blitz. Many of these witnesses were children at the time, but I have also tracked down a nurse who treated some of the casualties.

Alistair Lofthouse.

Acknowledgements

I am very grateful to the following people who helped in the production of this book:

Sheila Dawson
M Duffy
Brenda Nowlan
Ella Savage
Ken Atkin
Sidney Tanser

Anne Diver
Joan Mottram
Mabel Smith
Don Alexander
Eddie Radcliffe

Sheffield Libraries, Local Studies Section, especially Mike Spike
Peter Machan, additional photographs
Simon Dawson, additional research
Andrew Billingham, Technical Editor

Background to the Blitz

In 1933, 15 years after defeat in the First World War, the German people elected Adolf Hitler and his Nazi party into power. Disgruntled with over a decade of, what they considered, humiliation after their surrender in 1918, Hitler promised a new beginning for Germany. Although forbidden to have sizeable armed forces under conditions of the Versailles Treaty, Hitler's Third Reich secretly began rebuilding German forces on a grand scale. By 1939 the German air force, the Luftwaffe, comprised three million personnel of which 75,000 were aircrew and 25,000 were women.

Having to start from scratch allowed German forces to have the latest advanced technology and designs. While Britain's Royal Air Force had to contend with a force of mainly biplanes until the late 1930s, the Luftwaffe had the modern ME109 fighter, the terrifying Junkers JU87 Stuka dive bomber and the Heinkel HE111, to name but three. The latter aircraft was to cause Sheffield so much damage in 1940 and Germany could produce these at a rate of 100 per month.

On September 1st 1939, German forces commenced a Blitzkrieg, or 'lightning war', against Poland. Modern aircraft and tanks steamed through Polish horse cavalry within hours. By the September 3rd Britain was at war with Germany. Poland was lost, but there then followed a period of seven months in which little appeared to happen, this time is often referred to as the 'Phoney War'.

All was to change in May of 1940 as it was the turn of Belgium and France to suffer the Blitzkrieg. Britain had sent a force of men, tanks and aircraft to France, but they were no match for the Germans and, by June, the remains of the British Expeditionary Force were being lifted from the beaches of Dunkirk.

Now Britain faced Germany alone. Germany would have to adopt new tactics as the Blitzkrieg would not be an option due to the existence of the English Channel, a 20 mile strip of sea. So, a seaborne landing code named 'Sealion' would be required. First, however, the Royal Air Force would have to be destroyed. With the RAF gone the Luftwaffe could, in theory, sink the Royal Navy and then mount seaborne landings on the British South Coast. Thus, from July 1940, began what soon became known as 'The Battle of Britain' with hundreds of German fighters and bombers attacking RAF bases in the South of England.

British Hurricane and Spitfire fighters were heavily outnumbered by the Luftwaffe. German aircrews were very experienced having fought in Spain in 1937, Poland in 1939 and France in 1940, whereas the RAF aircrew were often novices, some with a mere 20 hours flying experience. However, the Germans were to get a shock for they didn't realize how advanced and organised British radar was in 1940. As soon as they took off from occupied French bases they were being detected by British radar. German aircrew were surprised to find that as soon as they crossed the Channel British fighters were there to 'welcome' them. The fighting was fierce with high losses on both sides. The German plan was to bomb RAF bases by day with fighter aircraft protecting the bomber formations. By September 1940, the Luftwaffe had lost hundreds of aircraft and their losses were unsustainable. The invasion of Britain was postponed initially to Spring 1941 and German tactics changed.

The change came on the night of September 7th 1940 when Luftwaffe bombers headed up the Thames estuary. Guided by the reflection of the moon on the water they targeted their bombs on London's East-End, mainly in the docks area. This marked a dramatic change in the war as, for the first time, non-military targets had been hit. The might of the Third Reich had been pitted against British civilians. Bombing would be concentrated in industrial and port areas, but a darker side of this new campaign was to eat away at the moral of the people; through destruction of their property, disruption of their daily routines and mounting casualty rates.

In the first few weeks of *The Night Blitz*, attacks were concentrated on the capital. During September and October 1940 there were 49 major raids but, from November, the Germans started to target other cities. Coventry was the first on November 14th where the enemy were trying to target vehicle and aircraft component factories. On November 23rd, Southampton was targeted. With its docks, oil installations and Spitfire fighter factory it was a prime target. Birmingham and Bristol soon followed.

The successes that the RAF had during *The Battle of Britain* were not to be repeated in the Night Blitz. Spitfire and Hurricane fighters had no means of locating enemy bombers in darkness. Small, light radars that could be carried in aircraft were rapidly being developed, but it was not until later in 1941 that this equipment became fully operational. The only defence that the cities had were the gun batteries placed around each one, but these failed to shoot down the enemy in any numbers. They did, however, boost the moral of the people by being a visible sign of the British fighting back.

Operation Crucible

Sheffield had suffered a few air-raids before the Night Blitz, the first being on August 18th 1940. Blackbrook Road was hit but caused no casualties. A raid on Sheaf Street on August 29th caused Sheffield's first fatalities when four people were killed and 78 injured. It was not until December that the full weight of the Blitz was to hit Sheffield.

Considering the importance of 'The City of Steel' the people of Sheffield were expecting a major raid sooner or later. Most of the city was devoted to steel, armament and aircraft component production. Indeed, the British Steel Coporation River Don forge was the only factory big enough in 1940 to forge the crankshafts for the Rolls Royce Merlin engines that powered the Spitfire and Hurricane fighters. The loss of this forge would have severely hit aircraft production.

The Germans often had a pattern of 'Doppelgänger' attacks meaning double raids carried out within a few days of each other in order to cause maximum damage in an area already thrown into chaos. Appropriatley the Luftwaffe named the raids 'Operation Crucible' in reference to Sheffield's pioneering history in the development of Crucible steel by Benjamin Huntsman in the 18th Century.

On the night of Thursday December 12th 1940 with a full moon, Heinkel 111s of KG55 commenced the raids at 7pm by dropping flares and high explosives. There then followed around nine hours of bombing where 350 tons of high explosives and incendiaries were dropped. Bombers often carried mixed bomb loads to maximise damage. The high explosives would not only completely destroy buildings they directly hit, but the blast would blow out windows and damage rooves in the surrounding area. Incendiary bombs dropped at the same time

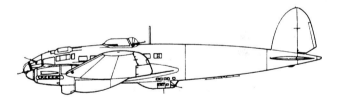

Heinkel 111, the most numerous of Luftwaffe bomber aircraft

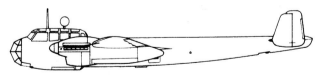

Dornier 17 bomber, less than 20 of these aircraft attacked Sheffield

would cause many small fires that would spread through the open windows and broken roof tiles.

Around 300 German aircraft, largely from Luftflotte III, took part in the raid.

Operating mainly from occupied France they consisted of Junkers JU88's, Dornier 17s and Heinkel 111s. The apparent targets were the factories to the East and North of the city, but the centre was the area most hit. Suburbs including Sharrow, Nether Edge, Heeley, Pitsmoor, Broomhill, Millhouses and Meersbrook were badly hit. The reason for the Luftwaffe missing the factories appeared to be a combination of there being ground fog over Attercliffe and Rotherham, and a possibility that German aircrews mistook The Moor for Attercliffe Road.

By 4 o'clock in the morning of Friday December 13th the raid was over, but at roughly 7 o'clock in the evening of Sunday 15th around 90 aircraft, guided by X-Gerät beams, a radio based blind navigation system similar in principal to today's instrument landing system, commenced their bombing around the Prince of Wales Road area. This time they managed to target the steel works, with a rolling mill at Brown Baileys being totally destroyed and a number of other mills being damaged.

During the two raids around 750 people were listed as missing with around 500 seriously injured. The official recorded total is now known to be 589 killed. Almost 3,000 houses and shops were damaged beyond repair with another 82,000 properties being damaged in some way. Many gas and water mains were destroyed and, more alarmingly, there were 394 unexploded bombs, known as UXBs, around Sheffield keeping The Royal Engineers busy for several years defusing them. Indeed over the years a number of UXBs have surfaced, the most recent being 'Hermon', a 500 kg bomb discovered near Bramall Lane in 1985. This led to the whole area being evacuated for two days. Hermon is now in display at the Kelham Island Museum in Sheffield.

Many people thought that the raiders would return, but they didn't. Manchester was the target for December 22nd & 23rd1940.

A German Me109 fighter that had been shot down during the Battle of Britain is put on public display at Sheffield's Barkers Pool.

The City Centre

This chapter takes a walk through Sheffield Centre from Moorfoot to Castle Markets. An almost identical walk is in another of our books: 'Lost Sheffield, Portrait of a Victorian City' showing similar views at around the turn of the 19th Century.

London Road

Barclays Bank was rebuilt in the 1950's, closing in the 1980's and now being occupied by a firework shop. The Co-Op to the right survived the Blitz and was demolished in the late 1980's.

The Moor

Originally known as South Street, this photograph taken the day after the first raid with an Army Bedford truck and dispatch rider parked half way up. The extent of the damage to the Moor area is evident today in that not a single building pre-dates 1940.

Atkinsons, The Moor

Totally destroyed on the night of December12th, today the store is the only independent department store in Sheffield.

Deacon's Bank, The Moor

In 1940 Rockingham Street joined the Moor where Rockingham Gate is now located. Many of the roads surrounding The Moor have totally changed, such as Penny Lane and Porter Street which have gone without trace.

Eddie's War

When the Second World War began in late 1939, I was almost five years old and lived at that time at 69 Southgrove Road in Sheffield.

At that age I wasn't really aware that a war had begun or, for that matter, what a war really was. This was all to change quite dramatically in the coming years. I enjoyed a lovely childhood in the old house which although it was terraced, it had been lived in by a well to do family prior to our tenancy as all the rooms had electric bell buttons which registered on a panel in the kitchen to summon the maid or the house keeper.

I began school at Hunters Bar Infants in May 1940 when I became five years old and began to realise that something unusual was happening. The most pronounced was the continuous testing of air raid sirens as they were installed in all strategic parts of the city. My pals and I would run around with arms outstretched, pretending to be aeroplanes, mimicking the undulating wail of the warning siren, then the monotone plain wail of the all clear when we had dropped our imaginary bombs.

The first physical signs of the approaching conflict was one day back at the old house when a council lorry arrived and a team of workmen unloaded and stacked a huge pile of galvanised corrugated steel sections in our back yard. My Dad, as a very outspoken and active member of the Air Raid Police (A.R.P.), had volunteered our back garden as the site for a large "Anderson" shelter that would serve about six households.

With my Dad helping, the team of men dug a huge hole in the garden about ten feet wide by twenty feet long and three feet deep. In this the shelter was built, half in and half out of the ground. I remember hearing Dad say "It's lovely and dry you know, our garden has a natural drain."

Over the next few weeks, masses of planks and boards, even huge railway sleepers appeared in our back yard. Dad had been what he called "out scrounging."

Dad set to and floored and panelled the whole inside of the shelter and fitted benches and wooden bunks. He fitted a pipe at the back, which prompted me to say "Are we going to have a fire Dad?" He said "No son, its so that we can breathe if the house falls on us!"

With the railway sleepers he built a massive porch around the door to prevent the rubble blocking us in if the house was hit. He then covered the whole shelter with all the earth and rubble from the pit and it looked like a huge rockery. In later years I remember him telling a neighbour that he had learned his skills when digging trenches during World War One.

During the following air raids, neighbours from all around deserted their own shelters to enjoy the safety and comfort of our shelter, which comfortably held about 20 people.

As my parents had been music hall artistes up to the start of the war, entertainment became a prime morale booster, and during the air raids we passed many happy laughing hours singing and reciting to each other.

Even today at 65 years old, I only have to smell candles and sulphur matches to bring back the memory of those joyous and exciting nights in the shelter and to bring back the piping voice of my then eight year old sister, Irene, reciting her favourite poem in an exaggerated Yorkshire accent, "Ey I wud like to gi thee a good cuppa tea if tha'd only come on't reight day. Now tha maunt come on Monday, it's weshin day", etcetera.

This was the camaraderie, which was to carry us through the hardship and fear, which was yet to come.

The fear was realised when my sister Irene, myself and my younger brother John, who was then only two, were dragged out of bed and deep sleep, to the undulating wail of the warning sirens and the clanging thud of distant bombs already falling on the industrial east end of Sheffield. I remember saying to my Dad "It just sounds like someone throwing dustbins out of bedroom windows".

There were many such raids and many false alarms and in the early part of the war. We had so many disturbed nights that if the weather was good we, the children, would often be put to bed on the bunks in the shelter, so that we wouldn't be disturbed later.

Fortunately for us in the north-west of the city most of the bombing was concentrated in the industrial east end. Many of the children were evacuated from that area of the city and taken into foster homes in other parts of the country.

Unfortunately some of the German bombers seemed to follow the Ecclesall Road route out of the city and often discharged surplus bombs and incendiaries.

As a result of this sporadic bombing a new phenomenon began to appear; bombed buildings and, as kids, we were drawn to them as if by magnets, in spite of warnings of danger from our parents. We spent many precarious hours climbing up shattered stairways and trampolining on half supported bedroom floors "looking for treasure" as my sister Irene would call it. We fortunately came through unscathed.

It was on December 6th 1940 that the real horror of the war came home to us and indeed the whole of Sheffield when Hitler decided to launch a massive air raid to bring an end to Sheffield steel making and arms manufacture. This raid became known as the 'Sheffield Blitz'.

To all of us at 69 Southgrove Road it was already a night of great hardship. First of all my Mother, who was heavily pregnant with my youngest brother to be and was expecting delivery at any moment. My sister Irene, myself and my younger brother John were all very ill with Chicken pox. This meant that my Dad who was supposed to be on night shift at Laycock Engineering producing munitions, was unable to go to work and my Aunt Muriel and Uncle Cyril were staying with us through our trauma.

When the warning sirens sounded, we didn't really know whether it was just half a dozen bombers attacking the east end, or just a false alarm. Consequently, because my Mother was about to give birth it was decided to stay in the house near to hot water and other necessities and to pray for safe deliverance.

The strongest part of the house was the cellar steps, between the close walls of

11

the stairwell, so it was here that we settled to wait for the all clear. As the sirens carried on with their undulating wail, the A.R.P. wardens minus my father were running through the streets blowing their whistles and shouting "Into the Anderson Shelters!"

Almost immediately we heard the high pitched whistling of bombs, another of Hitler's weapons designed to terrify the recipients, before blasting them to smithereens.

They were very near and seemed to be falling directly on us. As we crouched in speechless fear Dad, who had dashed outside to assess the situation, burst back in through the cellar door whilst huge explosions shook the whole house. He said "It's like hell out there. We'll never make it to the shelter now shrapnel and debris is raining down on the roofs. They're right over us." Even as he spoke there was a huge crash within the house and a bright glare shone around the cellar door, drowning out the dim light of the candles!

The door burst open and Uncle Cyril pushed onto the crowded stone steps of the cellar and screamed "Its an incendiary bomb. It just missed me. It smashed the front door in and is burning in the hall." I remember my Mother screaming still from the shock of the impact, as Uncle Cyril snatched a huge white woollen shawl which my Aunt Muriel had been crocheting for months ready for the arrival of the baby. Cyril shot out into the hallway and threw the folded shawl onto the hissing flaring bomb, which had the stench and ferocity of ten thousand sulphur matches. The shawl disappeared in a white flash of flame. By this time Dad had left Mom's side and I heard him shouting "You bloody fool, get the sand bucket from the passageway!

Just inside the front door was a huge heavy bristle doormat, Dad leapt over the flaming bomb, grabbed the mat and threw it on the bomb, then jumped on it himself. The bomb was extinguished, then Uncle Cyril appeared with a bucket of sand to finish the job off. He said to Dad "You're lucky, they sometimes explode you know." Dad said, "ahhh well it didn't. Thank God it wasn't a whistler or we would all be gone.

The shock of that bomb put my poor Mom out of labour and my youngest brother Douglas wasn't born until a fortnight later on December 20th.
Eventually the all-clear sirens began to sound to be met by cheers and prayers of thanks from all in our shelter.

As there were only chamber pots in the shelter, in a corner where nobody looked, I asked my Dad if he would take me to the toilet back in the house, which he dutifully did. We walked up the garden and across the back yard and a terrible stench of burning was in the air. There was a strange stillness and silence and it felt as if the whole city was holding in its breath.

When I had used the toilet, I walked along the corridor towards the stairs and Dad called me into the back bedroom. He had opened the blackout curtains and was looking across Broomgrove Road towards the centre of the city and the east end. He held me up to see the whole sky was lit up in a beautiful orange glow as hundreds of fires lit up the smoke filled air. Occasionally bombs continued to detonate in the heat. Dad said "It is a beautiful sight isn't it son? I want you to remember this all your life. You are looking at the colour of hatred and death."

Burtons, The Moor

The clothing retailer Burtons lost two town centre shops during the Blitz. A third at Attercliffe survived to become a car panels shop today, still with the Burtons logo set into the masonary.

Bombsites as Playgrounds

by Don Alexander

My sister, Mary, was 4½ in December 1940, I was three. We both had measles and my mother was bringing us from the doctors on the 12th to our house in Parkwood Road, Neepsend when she heard the first bomb drop at Stocksbridge. Little Mary had her new 6½ pence dolls set and a bottle of milk on the table when the sirens went at Andrews Toledo Steelworks. It was just half past six, my mother said it was the 'Purple Warning' and at 7pm flares were dropped to light up the targets for the Heinkel, Dornier and Junkers bombers.

Our road was a good target, surrounded by the steelworks, gasworks, Longden's wood yard, L.N.E.R. railway line to Manchester and the tram line to Hillsborough. The 'Monkey' pub (Wards Ales) stood at the bottom near tram stops and the entrance to Andrews Toledo.

My mother thought of bedding us down in our pantry since we had measles but my father, then a shell steel examiner for the admiralty prior to joining the army, went to the communal shelter underground in the woodyard to see if it would be acceptable for us to go there. Of course it was, which was lucky for us, as all our neighbours who decided to stay in their houses got killed, including a couple in their 30's, the Breedon's, who perished with their children; 11, 3 and 5 months old.

We were in the shelter 15½ hours from 7pm to 10.30am, Thursday and Friday 12 -13 December, a brilliant moonlit night. My mother recollected some humour, as well as anxiety that night. Harry Pugh saying he'd got Eve with him for the night, clutching a brand of soap called Eve. A four year old, Reggie Stone, repeated again and again: 'Hark! Bang! as the ground shook with the bombing.

Before we emerged at 10.30am an air-raid warden came with the grim news "You've no homes. They've all gone, Blitzed!" Every house was either destroyed or badly damaged.

Ike Crookes, on leave from H.M.S. Exeter, and a policeman became heroes by climbing a gas tank and putting out fires. My mother told me of these events many years later, before she died.

As for me, a 3 year old, I had slept right through it all and the only thing I remember of this catastrophe was a childish feeling of disappointment that our house, with doors and windows blown out, roofless but otherwise still standing was *not* a big pile of rubble to play on!

On Saturday December 14th 1940 German daytime reconnaissance planes flew over prior to another raid on the 15th. We spent that night in an Anderson shelter in the garden of a relative in Parsons Cross.

My sister and I had been evacuated before the bombing during the 'phoney war' to Castle Donnington. In January 1941 we were off again, with my mother this time, following a telegram from my father's brother, Don Alexander. He was inviting us to the stone cottage he shared with his wife Olive in the tiny village of Sewstern, Lincolnshire in the heart of rich farming and ironstone country, between Grantham and Melton Mowbray. We lived there for six months, returning to Neepsend when Longdens had repaired our house.

We were glad to return. My mother because she didn't get on with the house proud Olive who wanted to adopt me and teach me country skills such as wringing hens' necks! My sister was glad to return because she missed her Sheffield Friends and she was bullied by the locals at Buckminster Village School. I was glad to be back because I missed my friends and the village was so quiet! I was used to the noises of Neepsend - the comforting sounds of trains and trams, the screeching of billets being hot sawn, the crashing of scrap into pans, the constant hiss of steam from Andrews Toledo. Prior to living in the countryside I'd thought the night time hiss of steam was the sound of the world going round!

Don Alexander is the founder of 'Don Alexander', Sheffield Shop, Ecclesall Road.

Marks & Spencers, The Moor

Redgates, Moorhead

Friday December 13th, 1940 the devastated Moor. Inset, Redgates burns.

Newton Chambers, Moorhead

Soldiers boarding up Newton Chamber's wrecked showrooms pose for the camera. Today with the wider Furnival Gate it's difficult to get the actual position of this scene.

Moorhead

Three Horse Shoes Hotel, Charles Street

As the picture below was taken in July 2001, the new Town Hall was in its eleventh hour, being due for demolition in Autumn 2001. I understand that the people of Sheffield will not mourn its passing.

Charles Street

The Three Horse Shoes Hotel still smoulders. I wonder if the tow truck belongs to Brook Shaws whose building lies gutted to the right. Note early traffic lights, long since gone at this junction.

Little Pigs

by Anne Diver

During the Sheffield Blitz I lived with my parents and younger brother Harry at 696 Abbeydale Road, a fruit shop between Lynmouth Road Post Office where Jean Williams lived with her mother and stepfather and the fish and chip shop where Freddie and Michael Groves lived with their parents. Our shop is now a private house.

Jean Williams was older than me and took me to St. Oswalds Sunday School. Mum had bought the shop before her marriage. Dad worked at Wm Wards on Woodseats Road.

When we went to school on Carter Knowle Road we had to take our gas masks, which made us look like little pigs, in case there was a gas attack. My brother Harry slept on the camp beds in the kitchen, so it was not far to go to the cellar when the sirens went. Our cellar had been opened into the cellar under the Post Office. The Street entrance was in Lynmouth Road.

One night an incendiary bomb landed in the road and rolled down the steps burning a hole in the door. I saw it and, according to Mum, screamed. She pulled a blanket over me but I screamed again so she pulled it tighter and I stopped screaming. I was five years old at the time having had my birthday in September.

Mum had to go to Castlefolds Markets to buy supplies for the shop and she had to drive over the fire hoses still laying across the road. Dad was in the Home Guard and did his duty on Totley Moss. When the water cart came round he would wear his Home Guard uniform and go round the local roads telling people where it was so they could take kettles and buckets and fill them.

At school Mr Piers, the headmaster, made us write essays describing ourselves and where we lived and who with, so the Civil Defence would know how many lived there and what they looked like if our home was bombed. I can still remember my identity number KKBT 1783.

I can still remember the coaches going up Abbeydale Road after Dunkirk with sleeping soldiers. On Sundays we went walking with the Sheffield Clarion Ramblers and sometimes were waved away from certain fields because soldiers were there.

Brook Shaw car dealers, Charles Street

Most people would associate Brook Shaws with Gibralter Street, but in 1940 their showrooms had been more central. Brook Shaws went bankrupt in 1991 with Dixons taking their place. Their former site has been a car park ever since.

Fitzwilliam Street, Devonshire Green

The building to the right that is now the Forum was extensively damaged during the Blitz. By 1993 a new apartment block called Royal Plaza had been built on the car park where the City General Hospital had been.

Fitzwilliam Street

An interesting shot, taken some time after the Blitz with rubble removed. What was a large bomb site has become Devonshire Green. To the left, West One, Sheffield's largest City Living apartment blocks nears completion late 2003. It is however well over a year late at this stage due to a combination of management problems plus a fire in a contractors hut situated below the complex.

Devonshire Street

The scares of 60 years ago are visibly seen with the gaps in the buildings to the left and the fact that Devonshire Green was a result of bombing and subsequent clearance.

Adventures of a Sheffield Nurse

I was only seventeen in December 1940, not a 'proper nurse' by any means, but just about to leave the pre-nursing school to go on the wards to start real training.

I don't remember a lot about the night of December 12th. We had lectures and then back to the Nurses Home to study. But I do remember it started about 7pm and went on until about 7am.

The City General had no real damage that night apart from incendiary bombs and, of course, windows blown in everywhere. The upper floors of the wards were empty of patients and the ground floor windows were sandbagged. Inside were large wooden shutters which the nurses had to manhandle every night and morning. They provided black-out and kept the broken glass off the patients.

Only the 'top brass' were issued with tin hats, anyone else who had to go out had enamel bowls tied on with bandage. The thing that sticks in my mind, and more so as I get older, is the lack of panic, the pulling together with 'a let's get on with it' attitude. It's a pity there isn't more of that attitude today!

I remember enormous fires all around us, especially looking towards Attercliffe and Tinsley direction, but it was mostly the little houses and not the steel works. It was a glorious moonlight night. There was a searchlight battery at the end of Galotree Lane and another one above Roe Woods, 'Shire-something' I think. We could see the planes quite clearly.

We 'young things' were not allowed to go out of the nurse's home, but next morning myself and a colleague were sent to casualty as messenger girls (no lectures that day). I was stationed in the reception office with a list of casualties who had been admitted during the night. People came, on foot mostly since trams & buses were paralysed, searching for relatives. Many of them had been around all the other hospitals. Sometimes they'd found one member of the family, but still searching for others.

Casualties were still coming in and another task was to accompany the porter who took them on a trolley to the wards after attention in casualty, and sometimes to the mortuary. I remember having to carry a leg which was minus the owner, wrapped in cloth. There was a side room in the casualty department. Sister said 'You girls do NOT go in there' We did have a peep of course! Bodies waiting to be identified by rings, watches, etc, or what was left.

We were told that sister tutor, whom we considered to be a 'Dragon', spent the night around the hospital grounds with a stirrup pump putting out incendiaries while Frank, the hospital barber, carried the buckets of water.

As 'pre-nurses' we had the weekends free and I was fortunate enough to be able to get home to my parents in Wath-on-Dearne with two of my chums. We got a lift part of the way.

We set off back on the Sunday evening early and the Rotherham to Sheffield tram came to a halt somewhere in Attercliffe. It had started again; a bomb had hit the bridge ahead. I think it was a railway bridge, so the conductor said 'all out!' A kind man said "where are you girls going" so we told them we were nurses and he guided us up and down back streets, clambering over rubble until we got to Fir Vale, so we knew where we were. I don't suppose we thanked him enough for his kindness. We got into a row from home sister for being late in!

Those were the worst two nights I think, but there were many more raids afterwards. Every time the sirens went at night the home sister made all of us get up and go into the cellars of the nurses home, a bit like sewers but with hot steam pipes running through. We could have been scalded to death if we'd been hit, so afterwards we had to take our pillow and eiderdown and sleep on the ground floor, 3 stories above us. As soon as sister had gone we used to nip back up to our own rooms. We were very lucky not to be hit!

One evening when I was off duty, that was after I was 'on the wards' as from January 1st 1941. A friend and I went into town and a raid started so we set off back to the hospital on foot. Dashing up Spital Hill a man in a van offered us a lift as we were in uniform. Somewhere along the road, and I really can't remember where, he stopped and swore. There was a hole in the road surrounded by rubble. So he turned off and once again going down side streets dropped us off near to the hospital. I suppose we did a tour of Pitsmoor.

Brenda Nowlan
Student Nurse during the Blitz
Now retired in Lincolnshire

High Street

A dramatic shot of the Sheffield Star's office, Kemsley House, towering over the rubble. The burnt out wreck of Walsh's is on the left. Rebuilt in the 1950's, Walsh's became Rackhams, as part of the House of Fraser, and recently became T.J. Hughes discount store.

Campo Lane
Silverstones builders merchants has extensive damage. Rebuilt, the business survived into the 1980's.

Vicar Lane, District Bank

Post Blitz reconstruction has not returned this mock Tudor building to its former glory. The bank later became a branch of NatWest, closing in 1991 and having been empty since.

Vicar Lane

Seen from Church Street. The building of Parker Press, printers situated on the right was damaged and botched up. They remained in this rather decrepid building until it was destroyed by fire in 1991.

George Street, off High Street

Westminster Bank, High Street

Despite the damage and chaos a business man passes the wrecked Westminster Bank. Rebuilt post war the Westminster Bank merged with the National Provincial Bank in the late 1960's to form NatWest.

Night at the Cinema

My family had recently moved to the Abbeydale area and a Laurel & Hardy film was being shown at the Abbeydale Cinema. My elder sister, Elaine, wanted to go with her boyfriend to see the film and my parents agreed to let me go with them. It was the first time that I had been allowed to go to the cinema and I was very excited and promised to be on my best behaviour.

The film was great but, about half-way through, the screen blacked out. The audience was very disappointed and some people made whistling noises in disapproval, assuming that the film had to be rewound or that there was a technical fault. Then, an announcement was made by the manager that a bombing raid was in progress over Sheffield and would everyone make their way to the shelter underneath the cinema.

The shelter was spacious and soft drinks and ice cream were provided by the management, free of charge as compensation for missing the rest of the film. We remained in the shelter for several hours, getting more and more anxious with every passing hour. When we finally emerged from the shelter it was visibly obvious that the city had been bombed. The atmosphere was thick with black smoke and fumes and there were so many blazing fires lighting the skyline. For the first time in my life I felt real panic about my parents and couldn't wait to get home.

The following day we learned that Abbeydale Junior School had been severely damaged during the air raid and that there would be no more school lessons until

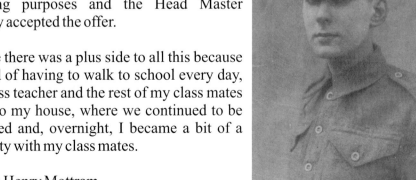

alternative arrangements could be made for housing and teaching the children. Local parents were approached by the school as to whether they had any rooms available in which local children could be taught. My parents offered the use of our front sitting room for teaching purposes and the Head Master happily accepted the offer.

For me there was a plus side to all this because instead of having to walk to school every day, my class teacher and the rest of my class mates came to my house, where we continued to be educated and, overnight, I became a bit of a celebrity with my class mates.

Austen Henry Mottram

King Street

Every building in this view was damaged beyond repair. The tram on Angel Street to the left is gutted. It would have stopped at the beginning of the raid, its passengers seeking shelter but, in hindsight, hopefully not at the nearby Marples Hotel.

C & A, Commercial Street

The destroyed C & A Modes was only a few years old being, completed in the early 1930's. Rebuilt postwar, C & A remained until the changing retail market forced the parent company to close its UK operation in 2000.

High Street, Change Alley

The Kings Head Hotel is burnt out. Change Alley has long since gone. It's a shame that this elegant building has been lost to us. A visit to either Leeds or Nottingham gives some sober contrasts to Sheffield of today.

Commercial Street

Just outside what was then and what is today C & A . What appears to be a corpse is, in fact, a manikin. A fire tender and two burnt out trams complete the picture. In all, some 30 trams were destroyed during the Blitz, but I understand that around half of those were later rebuilt. Trams were brought in from places such as Bradford, not only to replace damaged trams but also to cope with the increased demands of war.

Commercial Street

A digger works at the site of the Marples. Today a pub built on the site bears the same name. I believe that owing to post war road widening, the current Marples is in a slightly different position to the old one with the cellar, where the casualties were, being under the road where the single decker bus is on the lower picture.

Marples Hotel, rescue operation

The worst single incident of the Sheffield Blitz. Around 70-80 people had sought shelter in the cellar of the Marples Hotel. The cellar had not been intended as a shelter and therefore had not been reinforced as a shelter would have been. On the first night of the Blitz, the Marples took a direct hit and the building collapsed. In spite of a twelve day search, only seven people survived. A mere fourteen further people could be identified and the total death toll at the Marples was never established. During the 1950's, when the site was being redeveloped, wooden panels were erected as the builders anticipated finding further bodies as they dug new foundations.

Unexploded bombs, Chelsea Road

Its lucky that theses bombs didn't explode, the large one to the right is a 500kg and the two smaller ones are 250kg. The damage caused if they had gone off would of been considerable. After being loaded into the truck they may of been taken to a site in the country where they could safely be detonated.

Angel Street

An area of Sheffield that was generally destroyed by fire as opposed to blast damage. J. Abrahams in his 1942 book 'Sheffield Blitz' stated "Our stores and shops were destroyed because there were not enough fire watchers at that time to keep them safe."

The Bombing of Oughtibridge

by Sheila Dawson

Although the village of Oughtibridge is on the outskirts of Sheffield to the north, it did not escape bombing.

Nestling below the edge of dense woodland on the main road towards the village, stood a row of four cottages, Bland Houses by name.

One evening in an isolated incident these houses received a direct hit, resulting in tragic circumstances. Three people were to lose their lives. A baby was saved by his mother shielding him with her body. The mother was one of the fatalities. Three cottages were demolished, leaving an end one standing which, when repaired was inhabited for a number of years on.

Was the bombing a million to one chance? Perhaps not, for across a field and river was Darwin's Steel Works - was this the target?

In another instance, it was rumoured a bomb had dropped in daylight hours around the Gate Bank area, which did not explode. People in the immediate vicinity had to be evacuated, as a precautionary measure.

On another occasion a bomb was dropped on or near the railway line above the village, but not a lot of damage was done.

So although we lived in a rural area we didn't go entirely unscathed and many nights were spent in air raid shelters.

Sheila Dawson with her husband Douglas during WWII

Angel Street

Cockayne's department store is devastated. Rebuilt post-war and taken over by Leeds based Schofield's it finally closed in the early 1980's. The building was empty for almost ten years under threat of demolition for a shopping centre planned for the area. In the event Meadowhall Centre was built and Argos moved in here in the mid 1990's.

Angel Street, looking towards High Street

Seen here a while after the raids with the streets cleared and the damaged buildings fenced off.

Angel Street/Bank Street

Note the early style JCB to the right of the picture.

Rear of C & A, King Street

Less than 10 years old, the distinctively styled C & A looks decidedly unstable. Today only the building at the extreme bottom of the block remains.

B & C Co-op, Exchange Street

Another young building, the Co-op was a mere 20 years old when it was burnt out.

Biggest Firework Display Imaginable

I remember the night of the Sheffield Blitz vividly, even though I was only a small child. I was staying with my favourite aunty at the time. She and my Uncle Frank owned a grocer's shop in the Tinsley area. He was a pilot in the RAF and away from home most of the time and my aunty liked me to stay with her for company.

This particular night she had planned to take me to spend the evening with her mother and father-in-law, who lived at Millhouses. We boarded the tram at Tinsley and made our way into the city centre where we caught another tram to Millhouses. The tram wended its way to the bottom of the Moor and started its journey to Millhouses along the bottom end of London Road but, at the point just after the 'Locarno', the tram stopped and all the passengers were ordered off and taken into a nearby underground shelter.

Everyone was very composed and we entered the shelter in single file - no panic, pushing or shoving, but the shelter was very crowded and claustrophobic. There was insufficient room to sit down and I remember putting my arms around my Aunty Mary's legs for support and security. There was no small talk, just silence but, after everyone had time to assess the situation, people began to converse.

I could here a rumbling noise from outside the shelter which, in my innocence, I thought must be a thunder storm - I had no comprehension of bombs. The bangs grew louder and the lights went out completely and we were plunged into total darkness. A couple of people were carrying torches and this enabled them to look for candles, but it was quite a long time before someone found them. The banging grew louder and the walls of the shelter seemed to quake and then some of the plaster fell from the ceiling onto our heads. I remember asking my aunt for something to drink but there was nothing to eat or drink.

The atmosphere in the shelter was very dank and people were requested not to smoke because of the lack of fresh air. I don't know how long we were incarcerated in the shelter, but more than anything else, I desperately wanted to get outside, because my real fear was one of being buried alive, and I remember the sheer joy of being allowed to leave.

There was a total blackout when we came out from the shelter. The sky surrounding the city centre was aglow with fires radiating all the surrounding area with red, orange, yellow and golden colours. The air was full of black smoke and small particles of floating debris coupled with the pungent smell of burning and I could feel the heat radiating out. I was too young to equate the danger, damage or carnage of such an attack, but the spectacle was astounding to a child.

The light projected from the blazing city was so intense that we could see our way quite clearly without street lighting. My aunt took hold of my hand and we crossed the main road. As we looked back we could see that the tram on which we had been travelling was ablaze and the tram tracks were mangled and twisted, the street lights broken and mis-shapen.

When we reached Mount Pleasant we stopped again to take a final look at the biggest firework display imaginable and then we continued on our way to Millhouses. My aunt had been advised to avoid the tram tracks because the route was dangerous. Apparently the German pilots had used them to pinpoint their targets. We eventually arrived at our destination several hours later, shaken and exhausted.

The following day, when Aunty Mary returned to her shop in Tinsley, she found that a bomb had exploded nearby and all the windows in her property had been blown out and the roof had been very badly damaged.

I was, of course, totally oblivious to the fact that we had experienced a very historical moment in time. In retrospect, it was the biggest firework display I have ever seen and all other illuminations pale into insignificance by comparison.

Joan Mottram

Dedicated to Mary and Jessie Sayles

The City's Defences

To defend against any attack, Sheffield, like all other major manufacturing towns and cities, had various forms of defence. Sheffield, being the City of Steel was considered a prime target so it could be expected her defences were extensive.

What most people saw were the barrage balloons which were large un-manned hydrogen filled balloons that were transported and launched from lorries. These balloons would fly at a height of a few thousand feet, tethered to their launch trucks.

The idea was that these balloons would prevent enemy aircraft from flying low. If they did venture low they might collide with the balloons or get tangled with the balloon's tethers. The higher they flew, the more inaccurate their bombs would be. Also the higher they flew, the easier it was for radar to spot them and easier for ground based guns to fire at them.

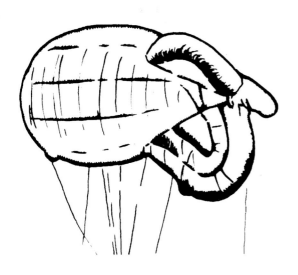

Sheffield's 72 barrage balloons were based at Norton where the driver training centre is now located. The site at Norton is often incorrectly referred to as Norton Aerodrome, however the base, known to the R.A.F as No.16 balloon centre under the command of 33 Group, had no facilities for aircraft but in the First World War there was an aerodrome at Meadowhead a few miles from Norton.

From Norton, each balloon would be dispersed to strategic areas of importance around the city. Sheffield had three squadrons of balloons; 939, 940 and 931 with a manpower of 1,000 men and women.

Next, were the anti-aircraft guns mounted on various sites throughout the city. Assisted by search lights, the guns would try to shoot down the enemy planes. In actual fact, shooting at high flying aircraft at night was virtually impossible. The Sheffield gunners were unable to shoot down any German aircraft during the whole of the war. To help improve the situation rocket batteries were introduced in 1942, by which time the Night Blitz of England was over.

Lastly, and more interestingly, were the Starfish sites. In Sheffield the Starfish sites were located between Strines dam and the Fox House pub on the A625 road, and also in Eckington Woods. The sites had large tanks of oil, tinfoil, lighting and apparatus to mimic the sparks produced by tram's pantographs. The aim of these sites was to confuse the approaching bombers, Sheffield would already be in darkness warned by Britain's radar network, but the Starfish site would be lit with flashes that looked like moving trams and mock furnaces. As the enemy arrived the mock city would slowly dim its lights as the real city would do during an air raid, then the oil tanks would be lit as if they were burning buildings, hopefully guiding the German bombers off their real target. During the Sheffield Blitz, the Starfish sites were incomplete but there are indications from other cities that the concept worked to an extent.

To assist the local population capable volunteers were formed into Air Raid Patrols and they became known ARP Wardens. These people would ensure that local air raid precautions, such as shelters, first aid posts and communications, were organised and manned. They would also go around the community at night ensuring that the blackout was maintained, that no light shone out from behind people's curtains. As raids took place wardens would ensure that everyone was in the shelters and would put themselves at great risk by being out in the middle of a raid. Their task also included rescuing those trapped and injured by bombs. Each warden had an area and kept an accurate list of who lived there to ensure that casualties and missing people could be accounted for. The lot of an ARP warden has been much immortalised in the BBC TV comedy *Dad's Army*.

At Bents Green, near High Storrs playing fields are hollows in the ground left by guns and searchlights located there during the war. The above hollow may well be where a search light was once located (inset). It was said that the vibrations from the firing of these guns caused considerable roof damage to nearby houses at Bents Green.

Presumably, as Sheffield's Starfish sites were mainly located in what is now the Peak District National Park, very little evidence remains today. Near Fox House, on the old pack horse road, lumps of concrete, foundations and trenches are the only visable reminders of the events of 60 years ago.

Shelter for the People

For the general public the government provided various types of shelter in which they could attempt to evade any potential air-raid. Public shelters were provided generally in the basements of commercial buildings. These basements would often be strengthened accordingly.

Anderson Shelter: Built in private gardens using corrugated steel. They were built partially underground for further blast protection. Some 150,000 Anderson shelters were built. Some survive today as garden storage. Conditions in winter were cold and damp and it was not uncommon for people to prefer to stay in their houses!

Morrison Shelter: Made from steel and assembled in a downstairs room. In the event of a raid the family would take shelter in this cage. If the house was hit then the structure would protect the occupants from falling masonary. The illustration above shows the shelter being used as a table. There were concerns that people could be trapped in burning buildings with these shelters, however, over 500,000 were distributed free and saved countless lives.

Reminders of The Blitz

The pillars of Sheffield's City Hall bear witness to the 1940 Blitz. Square patches of stone have been used to repair shrapnel damage as fragments of metal from exploding bombs hit the stone work.

As over 2,000 houses were destroyed during the Blitz in Sheffield there became a need for rapid new housing. The solution was 'pre-fabs' in which sections of houses could be made in factories and quickly assembled on site. Some of these short term houses still exist today at Stannington. One built in 1945 by German prisoners of war has recently been sold for £45,000. It cost £45 to build and had an intended design life of 10 years. Many of these pre-fabs were built by aircraft companies as wartime aircraft production ceased, hence much of the buildings incorporated aircraft materials not normally associated with housing, such as aluminium.

The Suburbs

Greenhill Avenue

This picture has been reproduced a number of times over the years, incorrectly titled as Bocking Lane. An easy mistake to make as both Greenhill Avenue and Bocking Lane run into each other. The house in the foreground was completely flattened and the site has since been occupied by garages. Its damaged neighbour has been rebuilt. At the time these properties must have been less than 10 years old.

Westbourne Road, Broomhill

Fortunately the house to the right with the turret has been saved. Note the white stripes painted around the lamp post. In the days of the 'Black Out' there were no street lights and vehicle headlights were dimmed. The chance of hitting objects in the hours of darkness were very high. Indeed, in the early part of the war prior to the Blitz, there was much concern over the 'Black Out' as the accident and death rates increased. Street furniture was hence painted with white paint to assist pedestrians and motorists.

Archibald Road, Nether Edge

The damaged semi was completely rebuilt as was its detached neighbour .

Kenwood Road

A massive bomb hit the road in front of this house causing a crater 100 feet across. On the opposite side of the road a gap in the trees marks the spot where five trees had taken the blast. No.40 Kenwood Road, above, was badly damaged and has since been replaced by the modern house shown below.

Sharrow Vale at War

by Ken Atkin

Early in the war, pupils attended Hunters Bar School during the mornings only in order that pupils from Pomona Street School could attend in the afternoon. Fear of air raids caused a number of pupils to be sent to Clifford School on Psalter Lane. Lessons were also held in various houses in the area, including 53 and 75 Wayland Road, and a house at the junction of Psalter lane and Hardwick Crescent. Hunters Bar staff at that time included head teacher Mrs Bingham and teachers Mrs Long, Laver, Hill and Cooper.

The Factory workshop at the junction of Sharrow Vale Road and Cowlishaw Road, now Gilberts' pine factory shop, was used as a fire station with the rear yard used for fire drills. The National Fire Service took water from Snuff Mill Dam on Sharrow Vale Road and a surface water tank on allotments in Ecclesall Road, now Tesco's.

Psalter Lane Bluecoat School, later the Sheffield College of Arts and Crafts and now Sheffield Hallam University, was used as a department for the Royal Army Service Corps. Allegedly, some of the local lads knew how to gain entry without being seen by sentry. St. Augustine's Parish Hall, Western Road was taken over by the army as a store for the duration of the war. The army also had headquarters at Endcliffe Hall, Endcliffe Vale Road and adjoining no.3 Kenwood Road.

Balloon barrage sites were installed by the Air Force in the field near Psalter Lane Methodist church and the field by the junction of Endcliffe Vale Road and Brocco Bank. These sites had nissen huts and a vehicle with a winch to which the balloons were secured.

Sharrow Vale Road had surface air raid shelters made with brick walls and a concrete roof in an area now occupied by Motor Factors and the flats next to the snuff mill. Domestic Anderson shelters were constructed of corrugated steel sheets for putting into gardens. Household Morrison shelters had steel table tops with wire mesh sides.

Water supplies were delivered daily either by a lorry with a large tank or a bowser and householders or their children had to queue with buckets.

Houses were supplied with sand bags for use on incendiary bombs, but several houses had stirrup pumps to pump water from a bucket in case of fire. A few houses received ladders for emergencies. House walls had painted signs to indicate that they had these pumps or ladders. Each road had several householders who were nominated fire watchers and, issued with helmets, worked on a rota basis for duty.

When the sirens sounded all were on duty.

The night of 12 December 1940 saw the Blitz. Children did not go to school for several days afterwards until suitable accommodation was found for them in houses or alternative schools.

Bombs landed in the field behind Clifford School, Ratcliffe Road and Wayland Road. These damaged roofs and windows of adjoining houses. One bomb scored a direct hit on 92/94 Psalter Lane which were occupied by soldiers at the time. Later no. 96 collapsed into the crater. Several boys assisted ARP wardens in clearing the house of furniture before they had to withdraw. A further bomb landed at the junction of Psalter Lane and Bagshot Street again causing damage to nearby houses. Other houses were destroyed between nos. 4 and 14 Westbrook Bank, and more damage at the junction of Clarkehouse Road and Westbourne Road.

During the Blitz St. Augustine's Church was hit by an incendiary bomb which fortunately burned out in the roof space. Its remains were found on the church floor the following day.

Several bombs landed in the Nether Edge area and one, unexploded, was found in the paddock of a house in Cavendish Road. I was present when this was excavated and removed by the bomb squad.

The 29th Montgomery Scout Group met at Endcliffe Hall. When the Army moved them out they came to the 59th St. Augustine's Group at the Parish Hall, Wiseton Road. When the Army also took over here they again moved, this time to the Parish Hall, Dyson Place for the remainder of the War. The Scouts took a very active part in local events with several reporting to the NFS on Sharrow Vale Road for weekend training on hose pipes and fire pumps. Older scouts erected Anderson and Morrison shelters and they were called back again to dismantle the Morrison shelters when these were required for homes in London when the flying bombs started in 1943. Scouts also collected waste paper, lead, aluminium, books and magazines. Older members and leaders, before military call-up, gave 'National Service' by fire watching City Centre buildings and staffing the Trippet Lane HQ which was used as a canteen for Civil Defence workshops. The scouts also acted as patients for training teams of wardens for Civil Defence exercises.

Ken, after illness, passed away in June of 2001

Westbrook Bank, taken from rear of Sharrow Vale Road

It is a widely held belief that bombs, like lightning, only strike you once. However at Westbrook Bank this row of houses was hit by a high explosive bomb trapping a man in a cellar. Whilst attempting to rescue the man a further bomb fell on the site killing 5 of the rescue squad. Forty hours later the original trapped man was released but sadly, died in hospital later.

Kenwood Park Road

Number 52 was the home of the Homer family. Hit by a high explosive bomb the family lost a daughter in the blast.

A new house was built on the site during the 1950's with the original Victorian gate posts being retained.

Meersbrook Park Road

Notice the person standing in what is left of the attic bedroom. I wonder if it was his bedroom? This extensive damage was probably a direct hit from high explosives. All the damage is caused by blast with very little in terms of fire damage.

Bombing at Meersbrook

by Sidney Tanser

In 1940 I was 22 and lived with my parents, three brothers and sister in Meersbrook. I remember the night we were bombed quite clearly starting with the awful wailing air raid sirens. We all grabbed our gas masks before dashing to the Anderson air raid shelter in the bottom of the garden, except my Father who was working that night.

The inside of the shelter was wet and damp and we huddled together on the two wooden benches running along the side walls inside. When the raid started the noise was deafening and the ground shook. There was an awful feeling of uncertainty and thoughts ran through our minds about a bomb hitting us. It was certainly impossible to sleep, but we still had to go to work the next day regardless. After what seemed an eternity the raid stopped and we were noisily gathered by the Air Raid Warden, who for our own safety, escorted us to a communal shelter in Meersbrook park for the rest of the night as more raids were predicted.

Early next morning we returned home and, to our horror discovered that the front of our house was missing and all the furniture destroyed. We went to find the local warden who directed us to emergency accommodation where we stayed until the house was repaired.

I remember my father saying how shocked he was when he came home to find his house destroyed and no idea where his family was.

Sidney's war years weren't just in Sheffield though. A year later he joined the army and served in the Kings Own Yorkshire Light Infantry as a bren gunner. In 1945 he was injured by an exploding shell whilst in combat. He was then transferred to the Royal Army Ordnance Corps and whilst serving in Belgium he met his wife to be, a Russian Doctor's daughter, Neli Brundelina.

Sidney survived the war and now lives in Oughtibridge, Sheffield with his wife.

Sidney and Neli in 1945

65

Burgoyne Road, Walkley

Postwar redevelopment has totally changed the area.

Heavy With Bombs

We were living on Chesterfield Road opposite to where Lavers are now. On the night of the first raid we could hear German bombers. They sounded different to British aircraft, a sort of droning sound. We used to say that they sounded 'Heavy' - heavy with bombs! A number of houses were hit around us. Further up Chesterfield Road, where there is now a small Police station, a couple of people were killed. Near to us in the post office a lady and her dog were trapped in the cellar. It took two days to get them out. The water was out during the first few days so we got our water from broken mains in the street.

Just after the raids I went to town. It was so upsetting, all the shops on the Moor were just a pile of twisted girders. Binns on Button Lane was being used as a mass mortuary filled with coffins, I didn't see any as the windows were covered over but everyone knew. I remember lists of unidentified bodies being posted up at Highfield Library. They would give an idea of the person's age and jewellery but many were burnt so badly it was impossible to identify them.

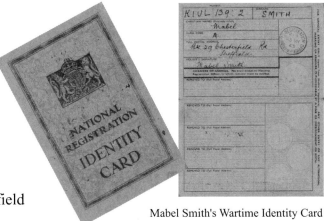

Mabel Smith's Wartime Identity Card

Mabel Smith
Now living at Gleadless, Sheffield

Black Budgie

I was only a child during the war but I remember a bomb dropping at the end of our road. I lived on Northlands Road, Southey Green. Our air raid shelter shook and all the windows were blown out from the blast. We used to leave our budgie in the house under the table when we had a raid. This night when we went back in, everywhere was covered in soot that had fallen from the chimney during the raid including our budgie. The bomb that shook our air raid shelter demolished two houses on Southey Hill. The next day our little black budgie died, it must have been the shock. My parents were upset, as people living near us were killed by the bombs.

M Duffy

Sandford Grove Road

The middle four houses have been totally rebuilt. The area is now a leafy mature suburb of Sheffield very distant from the destruction of 1940.

General Cemetery, Cemetery Road

The photograph above is labelled as Blitz damage 1940, however my records indicate this damage may have been a result of a much smaller later raid.

Ravencarr Road, Manor Estate

Today, all of Ravencarr Road has been cleared. The houses suffering more through the problems of the Manor estate than Hitler's bombs.

Granville Road

City centre on fire, viewed from Broomhall

In this photo, the glow of the burning city, described by two of our eyewitnesses can be seen. The town hall is visable to the left of the church tower.

Where The Bombs Dropped

The red dots on this map mark the positions of high explosive bombs dropped on Sheffield. There were too many incendiary bombs dropped to mark on this map. This map is based on 1944 records and has been updated from eye-witness accounts.

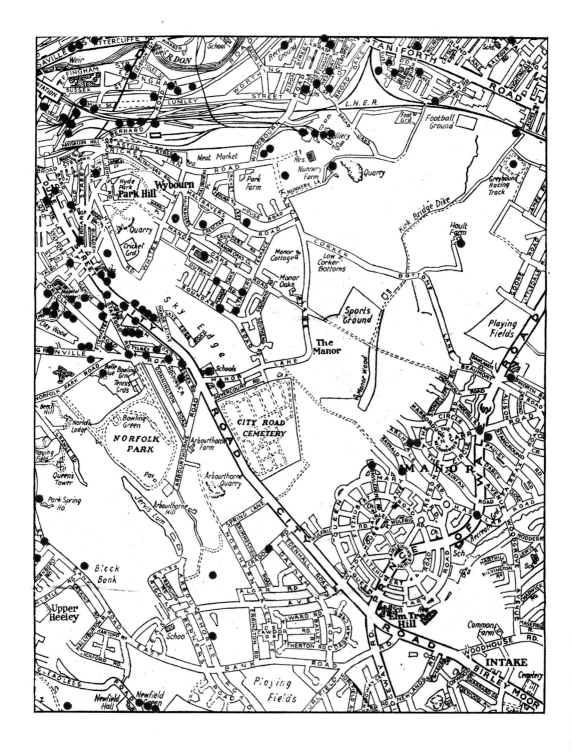